T0012108

The
SMALL and MIGHTY
Book of
Penguins

Published in 2023 by OH!
An imprint of Welbeck Children's Limited, part of Welbeck Publishing Group
Offices in: London – 20 Mortimer Street, London W1T 3JW
and Sydney – 205 Commonwealth Street, Surry Hills 2010
www.welbeckpublishing.com

Design and layout © Welbeck Children's Limited 2023
Text copyright © Welbeck Children's Limited 2023

A CIP catalogue record for this book is available from the British Library.

Writer: Tom Jackson
Illustrator: Isabel Muñoz
Consultant: Neil Philip
Design and editorial by Raspberry Books Ltd
Editorial Manager: Tash Mosheim
Design Manager: Russell Porter
Production: Jess Brisley

ISBN 978 1 80069 467 5

Printed in Heshan, China

10 9 8 7 6 5 4 3 2 1

FSC
www.fsc.org
MIX
Paper | Supporting
responsible forestry
FSC® C020056

The
SMALL and MIGHTY
Book of
Penguins

Tom Jackson and Isabel Muñoz

Contents

Feeding
Time
87

Penguin
Families
107

INTRODUCTION

This little book is bursting
with facts about penguins.

Penguins are seabirds that live in a
remarkable way. They have swapped
flying for swimming and now survive
in some of the coldest places on Earth.
And they're some of the cutest
animals in the world!

In the book you will discover . . .

- how an emperor penguin survives a winter in Antarctica

- penguins that live in hot places

- what African penguins have in common with donkeys

- why penguins steal stones from each other

. . . and lots more.

Jump into the ocean with the penguins and find out all about them.

Meet the Penguins

PENGUINS ARE WATERBIRDS.

They spend half of their time on land and the other half swimming out at sea looking for fish and other creatures to eat.

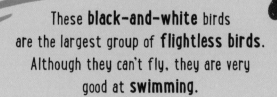

These **black-and-white** birds are the largest group of **flightless birds**. Although they can't fly, they are very good at **swimming**.

THERE ARE 18 SPECIES
(TYPES) OF PENGUINS.
ALL BUT ONE OF THEM
ARE ONLY FOUND SOUTH
OF THE EQUATOR
(THE IMAGINARY LINE
AROUND THE MIDDLE OF
THE WORLD).

PENGUIN SPECIES FALL INTO FOUR GROUPS:

king

emperor

1. LARGE PENGUINS: emperor and king penguins. They are much bigger than the rest.

chinstrap

gentoo

2. BRUSH-TAILED PENGUINS: gentoo, Adélie and chinstrap penguins. They have long tail feathers.

Adélie

13

3. BANDED PENGUINS: Magellanic, Humboldt, Galápagos, and African penguins. They have stripes across their breast.

4. CRESTED PENGUINS: macaroni, northern and southern rockhoppers, Snares crested, erect-crested, royal, and Fiordland penguins. All of these penguins have yellow crests above the eyes.

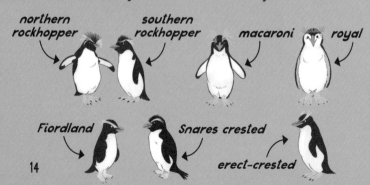

14

The yellow-eyed and little penguins are odd ones out and do not fit in the other groups.

~

They are thought to be similar to the world's first penguins that lived about 60 million years ago.

yellow-eyed

little

PENGUINS LIVE ON THE COASTS OF **THESE CONTINENTS**
(AND HUNDREDS OF ISLANDS, TOO):

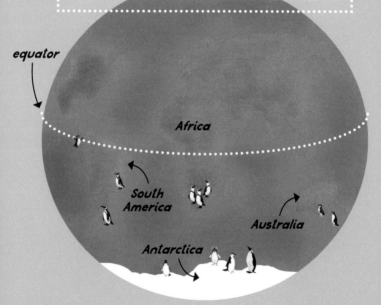

equator

Africa

South America

Australia

Antarctica

All penguins like COLD WATER best, even the ones that live in hot parts of the world, such as the Galápagos Islands.

Cold water has more fish and other foods in it than warm water does.

The smallest species is the
little penguin. It is only
about 1 ft. tall and weighs just 2 lb.

The little penguin lives in Australia and
New Zealand. It is also known as the blue
penguin—because its chicks have blue
feathers—and as the fairy penguin.

The **EMPEROR PENGUIN** of Antarctica is the **LARGEST** species. It is 3.5 ft. tall and weighs 90 lb. How tall are you?

19

The
GALÁPAGOS PENGUINS live
on islands in the Pacific Ocean.

The islands are right on the **equator**, so this species sometimes swims in the **Northern Hemisphere**

and sometimes in the **Southern Hemisphere** (the southern and northern halves of the world)!

THE CHINSTRAP

~ PENGUIN ~

is one of the few penguins to
have a white face. It is named
after the dark stripe on
its neck that looks like
a STRAP holding a helmet
on its head.

ZAVODOVSKI ISLAND
IN THE SOUTHERN OCEAN IS HOME TO AROUND
2 MILLION CHINSTRAP PENGUINS, THE LARGEST
GROUP, OR COLONY, OF PENGUINS IN THE WORLD.

THE **AFRICAN PENGUIN**

is the only species to
live in Africa. It lives
near the Cape
of Good Hope,
where the
ocean is very
cold and full
of fish.

Cape of Good Hope

The African penguin is also called the jackass penguin because it gives **LOUD BRAYING CALLS** that sound a bit like the noise a donkey (or jackass) makes.

African penguin

⌣ The ⌣
MAGELLANIC PENGUIN

lives along the east coast
of South America.

⌣ The ⌣
HUMBOLDT PENGUIN

lives along the west coast.
Both species are named
after famous explorers.

*Magellanic
penguin*

Humboldt penguin

The two
South American
penguins look very similar,
but there is a quick way
to tell them apart.

Magellanic penguins
have two black stripes
on their fronts
underneath their faces,
and the Humboldt
penguins have
only one.

27

THERE ARE THREE PENGUIN SPECIES LIVING ALONG THE COASTS OF NEW ZEALAND:

∽

1. THE HOIHO,
or yellow-eyed penguin

2. THE TAWAKI,
or Fiordland crested penguin

3. THE KORORA,
or little penguin

yellow-eyed
penguin

little
penguin

fiordland
crested
penguin

29

THE MACARONI PENGUIN HAS LONG, GOLDEN EYEBROWS.

Macaroni is an old nickname for **fashionable people** who wore **feathers** in their **hats**.

With at least **24 million** living around **Antarctica**, the macaroni penguin is the **most common** penguin species of all.

THE KING PENGUIN IS THE SECOND-LARGEST SPECIES, AFTER THE EMPEROR PENGUIN, STANDING JUST UNDER 3 FT. TALL. IT IS A CLOSE RELATIVE OF THE EMPEROR PENGUIN.

ROYAL PENGUINS

~

are one of the few species
to have white faces, rather
than black ones. Despite
its regal name, it is only
distantly related to king and
emperor penguins.

THE ADÉLIE PENGUIN is named after the wife of a French explorer, Jules Dumont d'Urville, who named the French part of Antarctica—and the penguins that lived there—after his wife, Adèle, nearly 200 years ago.

~

You can always tell you are looking at an Adélie penguin because the bird looking back will have a **white ring around each of its eyes.** No other penguin has this.

Adélie penguins don't need to come back to land to rest. They climb out of the water onto floating icebergs instead.

35

Some kinds of penguins
are very rare and in danger
of becoming extinct.
Many are being protected in
nature reserves.

~

THESE ARE THE MOST
ENDANGERED PENGUINS:

northern rockhopper penguin
erect-crested penguin
yellow-eyed penguin
African penguin
Galápagos penguin

THE RAREST PENGUINS OF ALL ARE THE YELLOW-EYED PENGUINS OF NEW ZEALAND.

~

There are just 4,000 left in the wild. The birds are threatened by cats and rats that people brought to New Zealand, which eat the chicks and eggs.

All penguins
are under threat
from human activity:

- Climate change is melting Antarctic ice, so there are fewer places for some types of penguins to live.

- Fishing by humans reduces the number of fish in the ocean, so penguins are going hungry.

- The beaches and rocky coasts where penguins live are being built on or are damaged by pollution.

39

Penguin
Bodies

Like other birds, penguins have two **legs**, two **wings**, a **beak**, and a **body covered in feathers**.

They lay eggs and have warm blood,

beak

wings

legs

but they are quite different from most birds ...

A penguin looks like it is flying
through the water.

It **FLAPS** its wings **UP** and **DOWN**,
just like a bird flying in the sky.

Penguins use their wings like oars
to push themselves along.

On land, a penguin finds it harder to walk around on its **SHORT LEGS**.

It has **HEAVY BONES** to help it stay underwater— not hollow, light bones like birds that fly.

A penguin's rounded body is shaped like a **TORPEDO** to help it slice easily through the water.

The outside of a penguin's body is covered in FLAT FEATHERS, which create a SMOOTH, STREAMLINED COAT.

The BONES in a penguin's WINGS are WIDE and FLAT to make the wings STIFF enough to push against water.

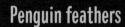

Penguin feathers
are coated in oil, which makes
them waterproof.
They stop water from
trickling through to a layer of
fluffy feathers underneath.
As long as this lower layer
stays dry, the penguin
will stay warm, even
in cold water or
icy winds.

PENGUINS HAVE FOUR KINDS OF FEATHERS:

1. The longest feathers are on the outside.

2. Small, hooked feathers cling to the outer feathers, holding them together.

3. Fluffy feathers grow against the skin. These feathers, also known as down, trap air bubbles underwater, working like a life jacket to keep the bird afloat.

4. Tiny bristle feathers are mixed in as well. These might be used as touch sensors around the body, but no one is quite sure.

There is a thick layer of fat, or blubber, under a penguin's skin.

This is another way of keeping cozy and warm in **ice-cold oceans**. The blubber also helps with keeping the bird afloat so it does not have to swim so hard.

~

Penguins keep their body temperature at around 100°F, in and out of the water, which is similar to a human's body temperature. Penguins can keep warm even when it is -75°F outside during the Antarctic winter.

Although we think of penguins as birds from cold places, some penguins often have to endure high temperatures of more than 85°F. To stay cool, Galápagos penguins go for a dip in the ocean.

Penguins
are mostly
BLACK and
WHITE.
They look
like they are
wearing a fancy
BLACK JACKET
and bright
WHITE SHIRT.

50

The black-and-white coloring helps penguins stay safe in the water. From below, all you can see is the bird's white belly, which blends in with the bright surface of the water.

Looking down into the deep, dark water, the penguin's dark back keeps it hidden. A lot of sea creatures use this trick, which is called COUNTERSHADING.

When a penguin feels cold, it turns its back to the sun. The dark feathers on the back warm up faster than the pale ones on the front.

～

Hot penguins pant like a dog and ruffle up their feathers to let out unwanted body heat.

About
1 in every
50,000 of all
penguins have pale
feathers all over
their bodies.
These rare birds are
called **isabelline**
penguins.

~

Some penguins, such as
king and emperor penguins, have
bright orange and **yellow patches**
on the breast and head.

Like other birds, penguins can see
ultraviolet (UV) light, which is
invisible to our eyes. A penguin's color
patches **glow** and **shimmer** even more
brightly in UV and show others just
how **strong** and
healthy that bird is.

MOST PENGUINS HAVE BROWN EYES, BUT NOT ALL DO:

∽

ROCKHOPPER AND MACARONI PENGUINS—red eyes

LITTLE PENGUINS—blue eyes

YELLOW-EYED PENGUINS—can you guess what color?

On land, penguins are **nearsighted**, which means they are good at seeing what is right in front of them, but things farther away look **blurred**. Underwater they can see very well.

While other
penguins have
round pupils like you,
the iris of an emperor
penguin forms a

diamond shape.

A king penguin's pupil
is a tiny square in
bright light.

A penguin has
wide webbed feet
with three clawed toes.
These vary in color from bright
pink to **yellow**
or **black.**

It is not a coincidence that
the bigger penguins, like **GENTOOS**
and **EMPEROR** penguins, live in colder
parts of the world, and smaller ones, like the
GALÁPAGOS and **AFRICAN** penguins,
live in warm places.

A small body cools down faster than a big one, so a small
penguin can't cope with the coldest places. It also
needs to EAT much MORE FOOD to keep WARM
and stay alive than a bigger
one does.

59

PENGUINS PREEN TO KEEP THEIR FEATHERS CLEAN AND WATERPROOF.

～

They do this by collecting oil in their bill (or beak) from a gland at the base of their tail. They then comb their feathers with the bill, spreading oil over them.

Although we cannot see them, penguins have ears on the sides of their heads, hidden under the feathers.

They can hear well and listen for the calls of other penguins.

61

Penguins shed ∼ their ∼ feathers every year,

replacing the old, dirty, and damaged ones with a fresh coat. The old feathers are pushed out of the skin by the new ones growing through.

It can take a few weeks for this process—**called molting**—to finish, and the penguins look very untidy for a while.

Penguins do not have much **fresh water to drink**, especially in Antarctica, where the water is always frozen solid. So the birds **drink seawater**, which is full of salt. Too much salt is bad for the penguins, so the birds get rid of what they don't need through grooves near the top of their bills.

◡

～ A ～
FOSSILIZED
PENGUIN

that lived 37 million years ago
was **5 FT. 3 IN. TALL** (which
is as tall as a human woman)
and had a sharp, 7 in. long bill
for spearing fish. It's known as
the **COLOSSUS PENGUIN.**

Penguins on the Move

ALL PENGUINS ARE FAST MOVERS IN WATER.

Most travel at about 5 mph, but the speed record goes to the gentoo, which can hit 22 mph. That is about the same speed as the speed limit for cars near houses and schools.

ON LAND, THE PENGUINS SLOW DOWN A LOT.

Their legs are short so that they
do not hang down in the water and make
swimming harder. That means on land penguins have
to stand upright and take only short steps.

Penguins use their **tails** as an extra support so they do not **topple over** backward. To walk they must **sway** from **side** to **side** with each step.

～ The ～
ADÉLIE PENGUIN
is the fastest
WADDLER.

It can reach almost 2.5 mph.

Most penguins only reach half that speed, and that is about as fast as you can crawl.

Most penguins do not travel far inland from the coast, but emperor penguins **make a long journey** away from the sea each year. Some travel more than **60 mi. across Antarctica's ice** to reach their breeding grounds.

EMPEROR PENGUINS TRAVEL
FASTER BY TOBOGGANING.
THEY FLOP ONTO THEIR STOMACHS
AND SLIDE ALONG.

They push with their feet and steer with their
flipper-like wings and can reach 6 mph.

As their name suggests,

ROCKHOPPERS

do not walk much but get around by hopping up and down rocky coasts.

～

In steep places penguins have to **grab the rock with their bills** and haul themselves up.
The wings are no help here.

Getting back into the water
is the most **dangerous
time** for penguins.

Killer whales or fierce
leopard seals might be hiding
from them **deep** in the **ocean**. Penguins
like to run and dive straight in so they
are at top speed and ready to escape
as soon as they hit the water.

As they swim out to sea, penguins sometimes **"porpoise,"** making **short jumps** into the air before diving back in. This makes it harder for an undersea predator to snatch a penguin.

Penguins have to "porpoise" so that they can breathe air as they swim along.

77

Penguins dive to different depths to
find their favorite foods.

THESE ARE THE TOP FIVE RECORD DIVES:

Little penguin
220 ft.

Human diver
(record without diving equipment):
397 ft.

Humboldt penguin
425 ft.

Adélie penguin
785 ft.

Emperor penguin
1,850 ft.

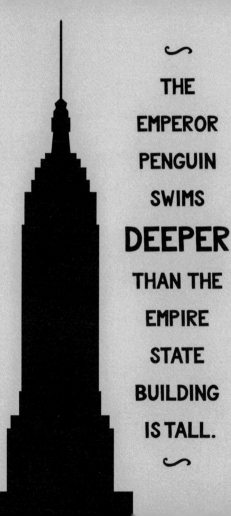

THE
EMPEROR
PENGUIN
SWIMS

DEEPER

THAN THE
EMPIRE
STATE
BUILDING
IS TALL.

79

Penguins have thicker, heavier bones than other birds, which makes it easier for them to swim down into the water.

80

The **DEEPER** the penguin goes, the higher the water pressure pushing on its body. That pressure squeezes out the **AIR BUBBLES** in the feathers, making the birds sink down even faster.

When it is time to leave
the water, the penguins
use their speed...

...surging
up...

...and out in
one big leap
and landing on
their feet!

After hunting, the penguins
swim on the surface by floating on their stomachs
and paddling with their wings.

Penguins can sleep out at sea floating on the surface of the water.

But most species head back to land for a rest. They tuck their head under a wing and can sleep standing up, or flopped on their belly in a burrow.

Penguins have to keep their feet very **cold** so they do not melt the snow that they are standing on. The melting snow would freeze again, and the bird would be **stuck to the ground!** A special web of blood vessels chills the hot blood going down into the feet and warms up the blood that is coming back up.

∿

To stop their feet getting TOO cold, emperor penguins lean back on their heels and rest on their tails so as to keep the front of their feet off the ground.

Feeding
Time

ALL PENGUINS
ARE HUNTERS
THAT FIND THEIR
FOOD OUT AT
SEA. THEY DO
NOT FEED WHEN
ON LAND.

THE SHAPE OF A PENGUIN'S BILL SHOWS WHAT KIND OF FOODS IT LIKES.

LONG POINTED BILL: Fish, squid, and other slippery prey.

SHORT, STURDY BILL: Krill and other small prey that are gobbled up in large amounts.

Penguins cannot really taste their food. Instead their tongue is covered in **bristles** that help grip prey as it is swallowed whole—and alive!

~

No birds have teeth, but penguins have rows of flexible TOOTH-LIKE SPIKES that poke down from the top of the mouth. These TRAP PREY, stopping it from wriggling back out of the mouth.

Penguins hunt by sight.

Their eyes see much better **underwater** than they do on land.

❧

Most penguins eat **shrimp-like** animals, such as **krill**. These little sea creatures live in **vast schools** that come near the surface.

Generally penguins dive to around 65 ft. to get the food they need.

93

PENGUINS THAT EAT FISH AND
SQUID HAVE TO DIVE MUCH
DEEPER, WHERE THE WATER
GETS VERY DARK.

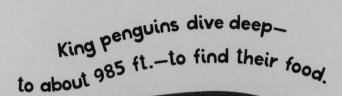

King penguins dive deep—
to about 985 ft.—to find their food.

The penguin's
**PUPILS OPEN
WIDE**
to let in more light
to see by.

Penguins also
use their sense of
smell to find food.
They pick up on the chemicals
in the water that show
krill are nearby.

Colored chemicals
in the **KRILL** they eat
make gentoo penguins'
bills **BRIGHT
ORANGE.**

When emperor penguins make a deep dive, their heart slows down.

This saves energy and oxygen so the birds can stay under for 20 minutes or more.

They hold the penguin diving record—some can even hold their breath underwater for more than **30 minutes**. Most of the blood is sent to the brain and muscles, while the rest of the body shuts down.

EMPEROR PENGUINS WILL SPEND SEVERAL MONTHS OUT AT SEA LOOKING FOR FOOD WITHOUT EVER TOUCHING LAND.

Little penguins are unusual
in that they hunt during
the day, then wait until
NIGHTFALL to come
back to land.

Rockhopper penguins hunt in packs, working together to **herd krill** into **tight balls** and then taking turns grabbing food.

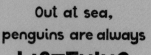

Out at sea, penguins are always **LISTENING** for the SOUNDS of PREY and **PREDATORS.**

If they pick up the CALLS of **ORCAS,** or **KILLER WHALES,** the birds will **scatter** in all **directions.**

The leopard seal is the main **enemy** of the penguins in the Southern Ocean. The seal **grabs** a penguin in its mouth and then **kills** the bird by **bashing** it on the **surface of the water**.

A medium-sized penguin **eats around 2 lb. of food every day.**

Macaroni penguins **eat more food** than any other seabird.

Together they **chomp up 10 million tons** of **krill** and **small fish every year!**

Penguin Families

Breeding colonies are very **smelly places**. Within days, the ground is covered in a **thick layer** of **penguin poop**, also known as guano.

Most penguins gather in **colonies** on the coast to **breed.** Penguin experts search for colonies using pictures taken from **space.**

Satellite cameras cannot make out individual penguins, but they can see the huge stains left in the snow by all the birds' **poop!**

The breeding season for most types of penguins starts in late spring.

The male penguins arrive at the colony first. They are in a hurry to find a good nesting spot to impress the females when they arrive.

The females get a few more days of feeding out at sea, and when they arrive, the waiting males will start to **call** and make **displays** that show how **strong** and **healthy** they are.

Most penguin nests are **shallow hollows** that will **protect** the **eggs** and **chicks** from **bad weather** and from **predators**, like foxes and hunting birds.

～

Nests that are too close to the water can be **washed away** in **storms**.

An area of penguin nests is called **a rookery.**

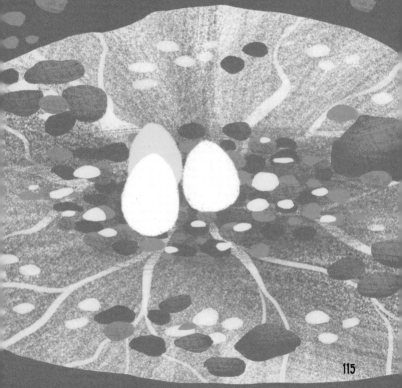

Penguins living in warmer areas build nests among plants that grow along the coast. Snares crested penguins live in rainforests, and build their nests among trees.

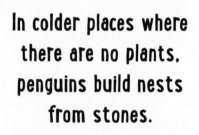

In colder places where
there are no plants,
penguins build nests
from stones.

Bigger and stronger males often
steal the best stones from their
neighbors to make a good nest.

A female penguin might mate with the same male as last year.

∽

She can hear his call. But she might decide instead to pair up with a new, **stronger male**. She will look for **bright** and **healthy feathers** when choosing a mate.

A **breeding pair** spend time **preening** each other, bowing, stretching, and calling together.

This **courtship** helps them form a **strong bond** because they are going to need to work as a team for several weeks to raise their chicks.

Penguins all lay creamy-white, pear-shaped eggs.

Smaller species, like rockhoppers, lay smaller eggs than the larger species, such as the emperor penguin. Most lay two eggs.

An Adélie penguin's egg weighs about 4 oz, which makes it about twice the size of a chicken's egg.

～

The little penguin's eggs are about the same size as a chicken's egg, weighing around 2 oz.

～

The emperor penguin's egg is very big—about 5 in. long—and it weighs 1 lb. It is still only a third of the size of an ostrich's egg, the largest egg of any bird.

Penguin parents **sit** on the
eggs to keep them **warm**.
They hatch after about
35 to 75 days, depending
on the type of penguin.

∽

After mating, crested penguins lay
two eggs, a few days apart.
The first egg is often smaller
than the second.

Crested penguins raise only one of the chicks.

Once both eggs have hatched, they **ignore** the **smaller chick**, leaving it to **STARVE** to **DEATH.**

Other penguins raise both chicks.

🌙 PENGUIN PARENTS 🌙
TAKE TURNS GUARDING THE
CHICKS AND GOING AWAY TO FEED.

When one parent comes back to the nest, they will feed the chicks regurgitated fish.

This is not a meal of penguin vomit. Instead the adult stores some of its food for the babies in a pouch in its throat.

When the chicks are older
and hungrier, both parents
need to leave to collect food.
The chicks **crowd together**
into a big group to **stay safe**
from **predators**.

As they grow, the penguin chicks are **covered** in a **thick coat** of **fluffy gray** or **brown feathers.**

This keeps them warm and camouflages them among the rocks.

It takes from **two** to **four months** for most penguin chicks to grow big enough to head out to **sea** and **feed**.

∾

Before it leaves the beach, a chick **sheds** its **fluffy feathers** and grows **adult feathers**, which become a **waterproof coat**.

Galápagos penguins

are able to raise chicks **two** or **three** times in a year.

KING PENGUINS
BREED ONCE EVERY
TWO YEARS. THEIR
CHICKS TAKE
ALMOST A YEAR AND
A HALF TO REACH
ADULT SIZE.

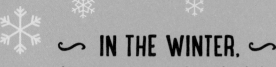

IN THE WINTER,

king penguin parents leave the chicks,
which are around four months old, on
the beach. Thousands of hungry chicks
HUDDLE TOGETHER to stay **WARM**
and **SURVIVE** on their **FAT RESERVES**
until spring arrives.

King and emperor
penguins do not build
nests. Instead they
lay one egg,
which is held on the
parent's **feet** and
kept warm under a
pouch-shaped flap on
their **belly.**

Unlike other penguins,
emperor penguins lay eggs
in the fall and incubate
eggs over the winter.

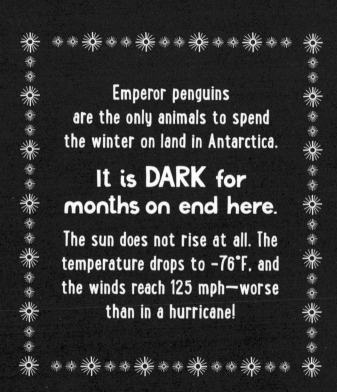

Emperor penguins
are the only animals to spend
the winter on land in Antarctica.

It is DARK for
months on end here.

The sun does not rise at all. The
temperature drops to -76°F, and
the winds reach 125 mph—worse
than in a hurricane!

Emperor penguins travel across the surface of the **frozen ocean** around **Antarctica** to a sheltered breeding ground, or rookery. This journey can take more than a month.

135

At the start of the breeding season, a third of the emperor penguin's body is **FAT**. This is a **FOOD SUPPLY** that the birds use **DURING THE WINTER**.

After arriving at the breeding site, the female emperor penguin **lays an egg** and gives it to the **male** to **incubate**. The female then heads back to the **sea** to feed through the winter.

The males **huddle together** to **keep warm.** Each one takes a turn standing around the **outside** of the group, where it is **coldest.**

If an egg rolls onto the **frozen ground,** the chick inside will **die within minutes,** so the male birds are **very careful.**

An emperor penguin
egg hatches after about
70 days. The father feeds
the chick with "crop-milk,"
a **thick, creamy goo**
made in his throat.

The mother arrives to take over when the chick is ten days old. She finds her family by **listening** for **their calls.**

The father is now much thinner, having **not eaten anything** for around **five months**. He heads back to sea to **avoid starving to death**. For the next four months, the parents will go back and forth to the sea to collect food for the chick. The ice is melting now, so the journey is shorter each time.

142

In midsummer, the **ice** around the penguin breeding ground is **MELTING** away, and the young emperor penguin goes for its **first swim** in the sea. It will keep growing for three more years before coming back to breed.